PLAINSPEAK, WY

Thanks you —

Joanna DeLey

PLAINSPEAK, WY

Joanna Doxey

PLATYPUS PRESS, England

First Edition, 2016

ISBN 978-0-9935321-6-0

Cover and interior layout by Peter Barnfather
Type set in Bergamo Pro, FontSite Inc.
Printed and bound in Great Britain by Clays Ltd, St Ives plc

Published by Platypus Press

10 9 8 7 6 5 4 3 2 1

In the old economy, where poetry taught us value, the self suffered as the world suffered, and the condition of the macro repeated in the micro-cosmos of one's life. In Joanna Doxey's beautiful debut collection, we find poems in which the global is also always the personal condition, and so we find in our hands a book of worry, a book of heartbreak, a book of disappearances.

Haunted by the various departures—ice, star, love, lover—these poems don't seek elegy's repair. Nor do they seek despair. Rather, as of the glacial erratic left bewilderingly in a meadow, this voice asks how it has found itself where it is, and how to speak of those forces now gone that are the only explanation of the mystery of being. But such is Doxey's sensitivity that even to say "ice," to say "snow," is heat enough to melt the remnant away. So it is worry turns back into care, and care opens us once again to those forces larger than the life that senses them: "I am done with faith but faith / is not done with me—"

Dan Beachy-Quick, author of *Circle's Apprentice*

In defining cultural geography, Carl O. Sauer famously wrote, "The thing to be known is the landscape itself. It is known through the totality of its forms." The gist of the schist is the variety of that totality, landscape being not only a geologic site, but the various habits and activities of the people living on it.

In Joanna Doxey's sparkling *Plainspeak, WY*, human and landscape fuse in the vast horizontal aspect of the western plains: "I want to lie flat on a flat land and border flat sky." Haunting, and acutely present, Doxey's poems pull at us like the ubiquitous Wyoming wind. Yet we are always a from and a to, a palimpsest of places and histories, present and absent, that fold space back into time. In this glacial manifold what doesn't globally inflect? Doxey's gift is to excavate the layering, to speak it plain and, in so doing, become a chosen place's witness: "Over the train tracks I have decided to be / from / here / or to be *from* and to be *here*."

In poems alternately spare and prosaic, Doxey scours the glacial path to find we too are missing. For *Plainspeak, WY* is also a book of heartbreak, and the vanished other who so animated by absence reminds us "this horizon pulls in silence." Always already, Doxey furrows the winnowed heart as an awakened, if provisional, recompense: "I need new words / or none at all // And / again // I cannot say anything for sure."

Matthew Cooperman, author of *Spool*

Contents

:   this land is a memory of wind without wind

Prologue

    i.

There is a memory of breath,
    or a relearning of pronouns.
I think again of lungs or glaciers without words

    when you tell me you are you again.
        (without — multiples)

One night you take wind from Wyoming.
I return to subtraction — back
    to a lost wind.

For what it's worth, I am layered
    in words

but cannot speak   for melting
    and the sound of calving we   were.

    I have been here before   :   body of fracture.

This makes "I" plural and oh,
    back and back to suffocate in such heaving breath   of   space.

Glaciers have a beautiful rhythm, one of massive extinction, one that tells of a disappearing history. The land that used to hold them is shaped by their weight, the empty land silently sharing evidence of their ancient sojourn. Consider a meadow, with an impossibly placed boulder resting at its center, abandoned thousands of years earlier by snow and ice, snow and the movement of melt—

glaciers in their absence shape a land that holds their memory.

There is an enormous boulder that sits solitary in a meadow along a trail we once hiked. In the summer when we prepare for your departure and move slowly apart, I cling to a dissolving landscape. I feel nothing but a later named *sadness* as we descend into the valley under a setting sun. In our concentrated silence I point to the boulder and you nod.

This is my memory, and so it is true. Otherwise, I cannot be sure.

In their receding, glaciers house a memory of time and accumulation—a vanishing history. Core samples taken from glaciers show bits of atmosphere, air bubbles that tell of ages past, ages before humans, ages that are disappearing from history as these glacial bodies melt and calve to their terminal end. Within their ice and snow, a space of memory and time. Soon, the libraries of cold will all be gone, a body of melt releasing an ancient atmosphere.

I miss you.

Chapter 1:   to write a history of ice it must melt

                                              there are ghosts, here
there are

         here: the sublimation zone
                                                    there is no Chapter 2

the terminal end of a glacier speaks of ice without ice   *(fluvial mourn)*
              silt is another word for ice
and I cannot get salt and teeth out of my mouth

Please: we listen to breath like cold   (dormant a while is silence)
there are icicles of conversation all over this town
in spring they will grow into cries of forsythia

I cling to wind and snow and I cannot get salt and teeth out of my head

I want to write of cathedrals but know only stone churches' thin hum
thank God for words: fragments of Wyoming make two

Bisected light is just land and the sole
                    of a melted footprint.

To interrupt light:
        bring solace in blue
        and a movement towards multiplicity,
        just two.

Or:
        the violence of boat to water
        and blade to undisturbed snow—
        birch branches work as well.

The reservoir froze in wind,
so watch the history of an uncompleted wave.

We are lucky to see movement in ice,
I am lucky for windswept silence.
A gaze and a winnowed lung.

The reasons of why
are seasonal   :
the skeleton of yellow
and our backbones.

I fracture again.

Words are sacred to me and you take *love* away, leaving a husk of a word. Within three weeks of depositing you in flat land you fall in love with a much younger woman. I tell you, as you leave me between states—your voice so distant and close like sleep—that I had never used the word "love" before. I wonder if, like the name Glacier National Park, *love* would always stand for something that had moved through it and disappeared. Would *love* always erode into empty?

Time moves differently for some people, I suppose.

I take to driving the perimeter of the enormous reservoir that sits above the town where we once lived. Driving south to north, I can look down on the entire town to the right. To the left, the mass of reservoir, black in night. Pockets of light from the houses across the way. I need the repetition of circular motion, to feel a pull to this land whose formation seems marked sharply by wind and violent movement.

I need perspective.

Book of Worry

The thing is this:

the thing is

      I want to lie flat on a flat land and border flat sky: look down
                                      upon:
                             press down:

    we are star-shaped, like this

    In this love of commas   I delete them

    We are star-shaped like this   planted to ground   I remember summer
           Wyoming   and I only miss autumn in autumn

I dream of places I have never been, but I dream of them often so they are familiar—

        1. here, I know I will calm into drown—again
        1. this valley where I do not love you
        1. this waterfall, and I am not surprised at the

    fall

In this humming and doubled land, hold worry, only me—

    and I get older or I grow farther from myself and I always most love
the moment before now and the history of a word like snow

: Wh

I forget your name

I want to live in flat lands and miss being nested by mountains
I worry you are not in this list

If I was to be honest, I would tell you I am not writing of glaciers
                                        I only worry of their memory
and plains, I can turn northward some nights (the horizon more distinct in darkness)
and from above this town I can—

My book of worry will remember you—

this is not a book of states, but just try to say the word *Nebraska* without looking up:

here—

but *here* sky and ground in steel and sky consumed snow   I am not concerned
with the touches of light and pink, but the sinking into the *closer to blue*

it is what it is but I need perspective

        This place where you can see mountains is not a mountain,
        perched tree / perched barn   they have been
        here before—I left circles on plains before I knew you, after you stopped

please just say it plain

I wrote this on a glacier, once   *I have thinned time before*

steel leaves out the stars and by saying color you can see it—
steel blue steel grey steel my eyes from the border of sky

this is the afterimage of a song, not the song,
I name it snow

We leave our town under a full moon.

We drive north through a windless Wyoming night. This is not the Wyoming I remember, or maybe the one I created through reading stories of the West, and from a brief visit to a dusty rodeo in Cody when I was young. The image of wind and the rodeo dust in my eyes have always stuck with me   defining Wyoming.

> This quiet land
> seems unearthly.
>
> I want to burrow into this silent night state and rest there,
> stabilize *us*
>
> there—

to build an isolated sphere in this night   with its stillness
and preternatural light. The evidence of past wind
etched: sharpened edges of land
pocketed by shadow and moonlight.

There is a history of wind—here.

I hold definitions of *Wyoming*

And in this wandering:
      home is sky between a latticed bridge in Laramie
      if the bridge was not   the sky would

Over the train tracks I have decided to be

    from
            here

or to be *from* and to be *here*

Interlude

I need new words
or none at all.

Suppose I had one such as:

       this horizon,
       this horizon pulls in silence.
       There is no denying
and
       I am drawn in again.

And
again.

This: land is the way I know love.
This: inevitable glance skyward and I rest
       into space and silence.

I am certain: there are no words.

I cannot say anything for sure.

Had I one.

I can bury a voice and name it foxglove or iris.

This pull. And maybe things don't mend.

My sense of direction is not a sense but the lengthening sun each day, a pull towards

light.

The sun is growing longer again.

(starve loneliness and it only thrives more)

No, if I was to be honest, I would tell you nothing.
                    Falling away from these memories differently, some nights—

              I remember time, once.

The states I erode burn and I hold them separate—this smoldering land still singes.
Move on   to loam and wind.

             This golden contrast with *Nebraska* sometimes breaks my heart.

Book of Absence: Definitions of Ice

I visualize disembodied wounds everywhere. They have a spherical body. They are grey-blue and transparent like scalloped ice in the face of wind. Signs of erosion are not erosion. My mind is caught in the sublimation zone where ice and snow turn to gas without passing through the liquid stage. The state of nonexistence. *I have missed something.*

To look down seems

       they just stopped: a barrier eroded into wind
              left impressions of music underwater, but

not walls

this   where

where loam remembers its intone and grasps water in dust and dry

        or was water

                    (a succulent sound, this soil)

Or, they must have had some other marker of distance and minutes—

I only love the silent *h* in Wyoming

The whispers like wind
dropped   and

if I read that land now, I would underline different parts, I would engrain dust
and veins skewed with rhythm

I would   seem
    distant

This understanding of time, of seams
This understanding depends on distance

                    We are

                    a faint reference to image now

In this land full of sky we read sky:

        degrees of rain or wind, and beyond calm and a breeze
           brings silt and sometimes fire
    and beyond   calm I am beyond calm beyond I

To calm: exists in worry

See also: the broken can break again like water

    : the way a glacier has worried and wound its ends into calving

Spill fragments, for example

For example: the infinite and finite seem so close   not untouchable, but we all
    have skin and boundaries

    : I broke my heart on a dare   a calming water

Book of Worry: In a Time of Calving

How to represent continuity:
1. circle
2. line
3. asymptote
4. the translation of thirty-one years is an image
5. the translation of one moment takes many years

over I over again and

massive color is not surface   but

        everything is not

We will not fix this problem of time and fracture:
1. an asymptote

            again misses and keeps

over and always moving but I am tired   (a list: a sign of fatigue)

I only see things as they are:
1.   please appear diminished

In a time of calving
it's tired out

: A forgetting

We are all a misremembrance
and I forgot the orange juice
because of the grey   through   birch
and   sky—

                          or I was cold,

and this supermarket is arranged

unlike home

and I am sorry,
but I won't remember the juice, just
the sorry

If I could draw these words,
they would feel it and I
would mean more—

a divide. It can be hard to swallow
and I must save sound for echoing
or disappearing.

I can think of the different types of ice but I cannot think to the scent of soil—

remember the length of winter then?

Prologue

ii.

I cannot count the night now and I trust my decisions to others
                                        (in memories of wind we wound still)

I cannot perform erasures on any land and silt and snow: they circle they circle
and I accumulate in lateral melt

                        please return wind to windswept icescape   in summer   where
memoried ice cleaved music from bone to form ice scallops of empty sound in two

Only a hum inflates like yesterday
I relish in synonyms not definitions to write a book of worry

A leaving again in *blue*, unspecified.
I wake to horizons driving horizontal
through corn — so see this
            and think *sky*,
        not the rhythm of ridged soil curved.

More precisely : my draw
and a sense of missing towards—
there must be a boundary.

For example : history
The history of ice is rewritten twice a year.

I write the word again wishing for evidence.

Such a noisy word : *silence*

I am sure there must be another name for it.

The crocus will speak only in harmonics—it will speak of spring under
snow

We become coordinates in distance   like grids of field and boundaries in clay

There is no past tense
                              only memories of was and ice
in broken to smooth soil

Now:

                                             edges of flat lands are circles
maybe
                                             and maybe they just opened
inland

I attend a photography exhibit on climate change, stand in the back of a darkened auditorium and watch image after image of disappearing glacial masses flick across the screen. Their sublime extinction is shown in different scales, in different images and graphs, all with the same rhythmic end. A beautiful extermination of mass and time.

This is my work.

My notebook is filled with constellations of words in the facts of my heart/break and I wish them to mean no/thing.

Saying certain words perpetuates their meaning, as if they enact themselves. Try to say the word *heartbreak* and not feel your heart break. Or, I cannot say *snow* or *glacier* without the weight of absence on my chest. The words I surround myself in describe my heartbreak. I turn to synonyms.

Step 1: Extract the word *sad* from my writing.
Step 2: Replace them with *fluvial mourn* and *sublimation zone*.

None of these work.

This town pretends to be a small town and I
want only—light   no—moonlight

and the elevation

I want only

           eyes and   *and*   a deep sighing
           and elevation
           even this   this sounds like wind
           and I am wrapped round such air

I wish you could hear such fullness
I wish there were only sounds for empty
                        or the memory of
I have been wanting to write the history of this town since
I landed, but this striation has more
I have only a book with the names of rocks, but keep one and a fistful of snow,
no, silt

For a while, I thought the harvest moon only existed in those wide open plain states and rose orange over farm houses while I said goodbye to you. What I mean to say more specifically is the horizon under a harvest moon is what I miss the most.

I am looking down now.

Behind words there were stars

obscured or faded.

The ice is many years old. If I

compared our books mine

is worry and wrong

and wrought and I

do not know you.

I am done with faith but faith

is not done with me—

Therefore: morning
Therefore: cling to history

I have run out of space but there is my skin
and the migratory patterns of everyone who moves like I move   in circles.

Perhaps I long for glaciers like I long for the past—
the inevitability of all.
I miss missing you and I long
for the memory of absence.

Language is the closest loneliness.
Which is to say—
we are very far apart.
What is the word I am looking for?
In search of the moon tonight,
I find a premonition of the past—
a new moon as it remembers *light*.
I am without empty—
I cannot remember it, but I do remember *the*
and different types of absence.

I discovered—through my research on glaciers—the flat geological landscape where you now live to be the result of glacial melt. The land remembers (through its enormous flatness, dislocated debris, and large glacial lakes) the rivers of massive snow that shaped it.

I will call it sad. I will name it heartbreak.

"Then, in February, I tried for words not about ice but words hacked
from it—the ice at the end of the mind, so to speak—and failed."

Gretel Ehrlich, from *Islands, the Universe, Home*

:   in an earlier and earlier spring I grasp my collection

Prologue / To Rest a While

iii.

My collection of ice is full—mostly of echoes, so of sound

Ratios of weight to sound
Ratios of time to sound
Thin fractures are easy

and I need heft

In a dream I've never had
this panning into the body
and I am done with the work
of remembering—
instead, I study time to get nowhere again.

I wish I could say something not real, just to use other words.
And the feel in the mouth:

        curmudgeon

        chrysalis

        chrysanthemum (and not mean mum)

        Ursa Minor

I worry when this is done I will have overused all the words I love.
For example: I cannot care for *love* anymore.

Please.

So close—
you forget a name,
only a color and a waking.

I am in a noisy

dawn, so I say

nothing but

weight

wait over
noisy grey and a creating—

I do not believe in hearts
but rivers.
I'm not sure which is worse: sight
or memory.

The Etymology of Sorr(y)ow

You will lose weight and feel heavy.
There will be voices of reason, daily.
A heartbeat is repetition. A circle.
A forest encloses, like rain.
You will have no need for maps in forests or for maps of rain.

I am really into the word *sorrow*.
So I have lost sight of it.

Time is breaking my heart or just breaking in halves.
It grows in circles, it grows in light.
Somehow, a wound. A sounding of two letters drawn out.
Eh. A weight and the half-life of a circle.
Winding a rain around a forest and we are lost.

Theorem

If:
    say a name aloud to know the weight of breath
    the weight of a name alone, waltzing soft

Then:
    there are empty syllables of empty breath
    say the word "no" to fill an empty room

The slow waltz of archipelagos:
    they will reach the forward step
    leading back they must

Or:
    I do not believe in magnets, this falling
    away from light, this cannot binary, this world
    I place no faith in circles and words shallow out worry

They have not known this slow-moving mass
and we only read in images:
    the shift of land from above
    the route etching from afar

Memories of Ice

A strange amount of memorization is nothing like this song.

The amnesiac feels the exhilaration of waking, moment after moment.

I have worn out a memory of one night. I have broken

a word, I have broken.

The most preserved memory is that which is entombed, not relived.

Eroded and reshaped and reshaped I remembered, no

recalled, The morning is the mourning is the mourn and This

morn is nocturnal.

The Last Poem I Will Write to Glaciers

a   sorry   I

cannot

                    I moved   /   on

sometimes a path
sometimes I whittled too close

I am a winnowed

                breath   a winnowed heart or mouth

I forgot the word for *love*

Noise: I am sorry
So: just the color of sandstone
          and goodbye

This world is too warm for plurals   so melt into

I am a—

About the Author

Joanna Doxey holds an MFA from Colorado State University. Her work has appeared, or is forthcoming, in *Yemassee, Matter Journal, CutBank Literary Journal, Tinderbox*, and *Denver Quarterly*. She lives in Fort Collins, Colorado.

Acknowledgements

Grateful acknowledgements to *CutBank Literary Journal* for publishing *Book of Absence*, *Book of Worry*, *Interlude*, and *Book of Absence: Definitions of Ice*.

This book would not exist in its current form without the careful attention and guidance of Sasha Steensen and Matthew Cooperman. To you, I am indebted. Thank you, too, to Dan Beachy-Quick for the workshop space and generous readings from which many of these poems arose, and to Marius Lehene for expanding my definitions of landscape. And, to Carlo, for the walks around the reservoir.

Many thanks for the perspective and keen design of Michelle Tudor and Peter Barnfather at Platypus Press for shaping this manuscript into a book.

Of course, always, for my parents, Barbara and Paul Doxey, for my love of snow, ice, and words.

Notes

Epigraph

From *Islands, the Universe, Home*
(Viking Penguin, a division of Penguin Books USA Inc, 1991)
Copyright © 1991 by Gretel Ehrlich. All rights reserved.

"Heártbréak *is a spondee*"

From *Bluets*
(Wave Books, 2009)
Copyright © 2009 by Maggie Nelson. All rights reserved.

Check the Platypus Press website for further releases:

platypuspress.co.uk